IT'S TIME

By Pastor Cynthia Blackwell

It's Time
Pastor Cynthia Blackwell, Author
Published by 1 accord Christian Publishing Ministry
1accordcpm@gmail.com
202 - 774-9944

Edited by Dr. Theresa Thomas and Shelby Walker
Cover Design by Shelby Walker

ISBN (978-0-578-33019-8)

Contents

Dedication

This book is dedicated to my parents Robert Blackwell Sr. and, the late Gwendolyn Joyce Blackwell. Daddy, you are the apple of my eye and have been the best father a daughter could have. Your support and guidance have always been appreciated. Thank you for instilling in me as a little girl that I was your "princess" who would one day be your "queen." The one-on-one time we spent together and the sacrifices you made for me all of my life especially for me to attend and, graduate from an elite college was greatly appreciated and, has impacted my future in ways we both never could have imagined. "I LOVE YOU TO LIFE."

Mommy, all I can say at this point is Thanks! It is because of you that I am ALIVE. You gave me life. You were my #1 encourager. So many times, in my life I wanted to quit at different task, but you kept praying and encouraging me. You took me to Sunday School and Church as well as laid my spiritual foundation. You taught me the importance of fasting, praying and how and why to pay my tithes and offerings. I promised you that I would write a book, so here it is, after all, "**IT'S TIME**." I know you are rejoicing in heaven and are so proud of me.

Thanks, mommy, for always believing in me. I miss you so very much and I LOVE YOU.

I also dedicate this book to my siblings: Kimberly (Kim), Robert Jr. (Duddie) and Annette (Nettie B). Growing up we did our share of arguing and even fighting within our house, but one thing for sure when we stepped out of the house, if anyone bothered "one of us" you would have to deal with the other "three." You all had my back then and I know you have it now, through thick and thin we are siblings. "I LOVE YOU ALL TO LIFE" and thanks for putting up with a SASSY, CLASSY, sister such as me, better known to you all as SISTER C and as Nettie B says the Bossy Sister. Your support through the years has been greatly appreciated.

I also dedicate this book to my MÁAT sisters Camilla, Martina, Lisa, Tammy and, Theresa, and the late Tracy Cunningham, founder of MÁAT. You all have been my pillar of inspiration, motivation, and, support. Your love, listening ear, words of wisdom, correction, chastisement and monetary contributions have played an important role/part of the Women of God that I am. It was in this circle of sisterhood that I learned what transparency, confronting, and communication is all about. You all have always accepted me as I am, overlooked my weaknesses and embraced my strengths while telling me truth in love. Sometimes I wanted to hear it and received it and other days I wanted to resist it and crawl up under a rock and never return back to a MÁAT meeting, but you'll love for me would not allow me to quit but surrender to the truth and embrace the sisterhood. Thank you all.

Special thanks to Rachelle Brown, Rochelle Hall, Tia Hill, Sonya Davis, Michelle Alexander, Danyel Hartfield, Adrianne Rogers, Monica

Royster, Ayana Padmore, LaTayla Palmer, and Sandra Voss. On numerous occasions one of you would inquire and encourage me to write this book. Thank you, ladies, for loving, trusting and believing in me. You all have always seen the BEST in ME and Believed in Me. I couldn't have done it without your friendship and prayers.

I would be amiss if I did not honor and, acknowledge my two mighty prayer partners. I refer to them as my front-line intercessors and, warriors who helped me break through barriers, generational curses, strongholds, and, deal with spiritual and natural truths. Shanta Carpenter and Iris Tate, I Love the both of you to LIFE.

Introduction

We all know that in this day and **TIME**, if you want to know something all you have to do is search for it.

As I sat on my bed, while in deep reflection one day, it came to me to ask God exactly...what is **TIME**, after all our God is timeless! The word of God speaks of **TIME** in Ecclesiastes 3:1 this way; there is a time for everything. **TIME** is a indefinite progression of the existence and events that occur from the past through the present to the future.

Upon reflecting on this definition, I began to examine and re-visit the events of my 53 years on this earth from childhood to adolescence to adulthood, which made me realize I needed to write this book. One of my best friends said, "I have more days behind me than I do ahead of me." So, what have I done and what will I do with the time God has given me? What I am sure of right now is the fact that in this season of my life, God has birthed this book called "**IT"S TIME.**"

This book was inspired by the Holy Spirit, to motivate and encourage you to use and set aside **TIME** to seek God about His purpose for your life. Why may be the question you are now asking yourself. My answer to you, because **IT'S TIME**.

My purpose for writing this book was to inspire, to share my life's ups and downs...which includes a few defeats, many mistakes, a few failures, victories and successes. It is my hope and prayer that you will continue to move forward in **TIME** and obtain all that God has designed for you.

Are you ready to journey with me through **TIME**? Ready or not here it is. "**IT'S TIME**".

Chapter 1
It's Time

The word of God in Ecclesiastes 3:1 says there is a **TIME** and a season for everything and with this **TIME** comes purpose. "There is a time to be born and a time to die, a time to weep and a time to laugh" (Ecclesiastes 3:2 and 4).

As the verses continue through to verse eight, they continue to speak to my LIFE. My great grandmother the late Dora Pegues would say "it is just the way it is!" One day as my great grandmother and I were talking I began to ask her all kinds of questions (all pertaining to life). Some she answered, some she didn't, but I remember her saying "sugar just keep on living and as you do, all those questions will get answered in **TIME**, just keep living."

Oh, how right she was when she said, "**TIME** has a way of teaching us life lessons that will make it both bitter and sweet depending on the situations at the **TIME**." What I have learned is that no matter what I go through, I know and am assured that according to Romans 8:28, "...all things work together for good to those that love God, to those who are called according to His purpose."

No matter how many scriptures my mom and grandmothers made me memorize and quote or how many times I attended church, no matter how much I prayed, one thing was for sure, **TIME** waits for no one! I am persuaded that GOD is real, that he loves me so much, that he sent his only begotten son (Jesus) to the cross to die for my sins to reassure us that God loves me and you. He has a plan and purpose for our lives. God desires that no one would perish but all have everlasting life. (John 10: 28-30).

Now I know that God loves me in spite of my mistakes, failures, and the pain and hurt I caused others. He loves me unconditionally! You see, until I truly believed this, comprehended and applied this to my life, I was going to continue to make the same mistakes and fall into the same traps of hurting people. The devil is my enemy and yours too. I dare to say, we are often our own worst enemy, as well as the prince of darkness that is spoken of in Ephesians 6:12. His job is to kill and steal our joy, hopes, passions and dreams. He does not want us to obtain the eternal life that is promised to those who believe that Jesus Christ is God in the flesh. He wants us walking, living, and looking defeated. **IT'S TIME** to stop allowing and accepting everything the enemy throws our way. The word of God says he has given us power over the enemy (Luke 10:19). **IT'S TIME** for us to utilize our God-given power.

God has patiently revealed to me that His Word spoken through me has power. In Proverbs 18:21 God has said “The tongue has the power of life and death, and those who love it will eat it's fruit" (New International Leadership Bible). God revealed His power to me through scripture. As I kept reading and praying His word became alive to me so much so that it became a part of my daily routine to get up and get in God's word and presence. I must admit, there were days I didn't want to pray or read. God knew it but He loved me anyway. He answered prayers and sent people to love and understand me even with all my flaws. I have come to know and believe that can't nobody do me like Jesus. His love for me is unconditional and patient. He revealed this power to me through scripture...so patiently. I had a very bad temper, and I would speak to anybody and tell them what I wanted without considering how it sounded or who I was speaking to. It could have been a supervisor, leadership in the church, a police officer, a teacher or principal, a doctor or even an executive director. At the **TIME** it really didn't matter to me. Yet I was still professing to be a child of God and my conduct, conversation and behavior did not reflect what I was reading in the word of God. I was speaking and communicating as if I were the daughter of the devil.

God was tolerant with me because there were times when I was un-disciplined and my tone, tongue, temper, and attitude cost me jobs. Yes, that's right I was terminated at one job, and I walked off another without even thinking, or considering that when I applied for another job, I needed references or a background check. Yet, God still blessed me with good paying jobs.

One day, God got a hold of me and began to speak to me about being "nice/nasty" and how he was not pleased with my behavior/conversations to others. Through my many tears shed, God began a work in me called humility. He began to show me the faces of people that I needed to apologize to. This was very hard because He showed me, I was operating in pride. It was then and only then I got on my knees and lifted my hands to surrender. Realizing that my arms were too short to box with God, I needed to get free, repent and apologize! At this point I didn't care who saw me or what they thought. My greatest conviction now was to obey the voice of God and seek out those I have hurt to ask for their forgiveness. With God's help I began the process of seeking and contacting people which became my inner most assignment and priority at which **TIME** I began to apologize to all those that would accept my apologies.

I can now testify that there were still times when I would respond with a sharp response and had to be dealt with through the conviction of the Holy Spirit, but God was always patient with me.

In God's divine patience, I testify that there were still times of course, where I still had that sharp tongue and again the Holy Spirit had to convict me.

After enrolling in an anger management class and reading books such as "Anger is a Choice" and "30 Days to Taming Your Tongue," God then directed me to join another church where He showed me that accountability was what I desperately needed while on this Christian journey. This new process would allow me to become more like Him. Painfully, in **TIME,** I did learn how to identify my triggers. It was **TIME** to stop making excuses for why I said and did things in haste.

As you read this book, take the **TIME** to pause and reflect on the things that are causing you to say things out of your mouth that you will later regret. Words are powerful and you can't take them back after they have already been said.

Words are so powerful; they can cause a situation to turn from life to death or death to life (Proverbs 18:21 NILB). Watch what you are saying because it could be harmful once you have said it. If you would take notice back to my dedication page, there I stated, I loved my father and my siblings to **LIFE,** not declaring that I love them to **death**. When you have a headache, don't say my head is "killing me" you are speaking clots and tumors over yourself. It's better to say I have a headache. Please, be aware of what you are saying.

There was a very powerful man of God who Pastored God's flock. For years he would speak of his time of death, jokingly speaking of how people would come to view his body. All of a sudden, I get a call that he died. To this day I truly feel that his death was premature due to his own words that held power, not really realizing that he spoke death **TIME** and **TIME** again upon himself.

The truth is sometimes hard to deal with. For this reason, some reading this (I've lost) because I speak candidly. Others may wonder why this was written but know that my assignment here is to only cause you to focus on a shift in your language pattern and to bring attention to the way you may say things. For those of you that need to take a moment to repent for some things you may have spoken, there is a word of prayer God has given to me that you can also pray.

"Most gracious heavenly father please forgive me for speaking death, gloom and destruction. I repent for saying...(you fill in the blank). Thank you, father, for forgiving me and please help me be mindful of what I am speaking. “Let my conversations be pleasing in your sight according to your word in Psalm 19:14."

Bless God, if I may help someone who may be stuck or unaware. **IT'S TIME** for the body of believers and people in general to stop placing leaders such as Pastors, Apostles, Police Officers, Judges, Lawyers, on pedestals. They are simply children of God who are men and women with a title. These people are human, with human emotions and will make mistakes because of the Adamic sinful nature! However, mercy and grace will be their bodyguards if they seek God and keep a repentant heart. Bottom line, they are not your God; stop making them to be your God and seek the true living God who can determine if you will spend eternity in **HEAVEN or HELL**.

IT'S TIME to seek the LORD while he can be found. This seeking is not just to be on Sunday morning or during the week at bible studies.

Seeking of the Lord requires a disciplined lifestyle 24/7. When you start seeking Him you won't need to make a public announcement because your inward change will show on the outside, through your conversation, character, and conduct.

Chapter 2
In the Beginning

The word of God speaks to us that in the beginning (Genesis 1:1) that God created the heavens and the earth by speaking His word and the New Testament confirms in the book of (John Chapter 1:1-4) that the Word was with God...that was the light of Christ who would appear in the beginning with God...creating all things. The Word was God.

With this thought in mind let us consider our creation **TIME** in our mother's wound where God conceived us. When our mothers carried us, their diet, their mental state, their physical state was very detrimental to our development and delivery. If your mother was calm and peaceful, then you could possibly be also calm and peaceful, if she suffered with anxiety while carrying you or had diseases it could have affected your character and development or may even have been passed onto you as a generational curse. Meaning, if she dealt with a lot of stress and/or anger while carrying you then you could possibly be angry as well. It is very important to identify with the things that may have occurred in our development while in the wound as well as outside of the wound.

Maybe somewhere in your childhood or adolescence you were molested/raped and you never told anyone about it or you told someone and nothing was ever done about it. If you were violated and it was never dealt with or violated by more than one person on more than one occasion, these situations have an impact on your life. These horrific situations just may hinder your future relationships and choices. No parent in their absence wants to discover that their son or daughter was violated when they trusted the people they left them with.

Let us consider those who have been rejected at birth, who are reading this book at the present **TIME**, and perhaps rejection happened because the mother was raped, had a one-night stand or this was her first sexual encounter with someone was not a pleasant one where she became pregnant. Whatever the situation, a child that feels rejected from birth will go through emotional challenges in life. This can cause each encounter while growing up to feel rejection again and again that they carry through stages of life until they have an experience with God and allow Him to heal and deliver them. However, until then, they believe that teachers, coaches, supervisors and even pastors and members of their own families are all rejecting them at the slightest encounter.

Should you be one that has felt rejected by your mother or father, my heart goes out to you in prayer. May I suggest the first step to healing and recovery is found in acknowledgement and forgiveness. Some people may need to have a conversation with those who are still alive. Others may need to pray and forgive them in their heart. This is a painful process, but you must do it so you can close the door of rejection. Things that are never dealt with will fester in many areas of our lives. The enemy's job is to keep you bound, embarrassed and afraid to talk about it and confront it. Let us consider now what we may need to acknowledge that has occurred in our lives that possibly made us feel rejected, angry or bitter. Are there times when you are still running because you feel rejected? How many choices, decisions or relationships did you begin, leave or walk away from because of a former issue of rejection or anger? **IT'S TIME** for your healing, **IT'S TIME** for your deliverance, and **IT'S TIME** to be made free in your mind, in your heart and your emotions. I find that GOD IS ENOUGH to do just that.

Jesus had a converted physician walking with him by the name of Luke (Colossians 4:14). This is mentioned to assure you that it is okay to seek Godly Christian counsel to help you get through this process of healing.

The author of Journey to the Kingdom of God wrote that "few people want to deal with the fact that spirits are real" (Walker, 2020). These spirits continue from generation to generation until someone in the family gives their life to Christ through becoming a new creation. The curse is then broken. **IT'S TIME** to break these family curses! **IT'S TIME** to ask God to forgive us of our sins! "Breaking the family curse ends in the same place it began, in the family" (Walker, 2020).

Chapter 3
Time in Childhood, Adolescence and Adulthood

I can remember things from the age of three. I've always been a daddy's girl, remembering my mom being sick, in and out of the hospital and being cared for by my grandmothers (paternal and maternal) as well as my aunt. It came to me at that **TIME**, when my aunt left for college before Nettie B was born, I had been the baby of the family for seven years. By my own testimony, I was spoiled rotten, always having my way. How many of you know that is not a good thing? I found out the hard way after moving to DC, people did not treat me like daddy. I realized, quickly that it was no longer about me having my way, nor did anyone care about my feelings.

The **TIME** I spent in elementary, middle and high school my grades remained great and I became the teacher's pet. My uncle and aunts on both my mother and father's side of the family always treated me like a princess. I could do anything wrong. My mother was the disciplinarian in our house, and she stressed the importance of obtaining a great education. Along with weekly chores, I was rewarded with every toy a child could dream of. When anyone would come to the Blackwell's house at Christmas, they discovered that my siblings as well as myself never lacked anything. Every summer we took family vacations and on holidays we would spend time with our cousins.

During the **TIME** of my adolescent years, God developed in me a love for basketball and began perfecting that skill within me. This ability allowed me to play in High School as well as College, where I held the statistical record of obtaining the most rebounds at Mount Union College for years. My senior year in college, I injured my left knee and had to have surgery. After that **TIME,** I would never play basketball again. Eventually, after I relocated to Washington DC, I developed asthma and a severe case of eczema which on many numerous occasions, caused me to be in and out emergency rooms and Asthma clinics. After this, a **TIME** came when I entered into depression, not realizing that I was really home sick, I knew that going home was not an option for me even though my parents would have allowed me to come home. By this **TIME**, I had become very independent and determined to make it on my own.

To people reading this book, I have come to realize that depression came from not being able to do what I loved...I couldn't play basketball unless at the time I committed to wearing a knee brace that was specifically designed for me. In addition to that, I didn’t know of any leagues in the area, didn't have a car yet and had to depend on public transportation which was new for me coming from little Farrell, Pennsylvania (PA). All I knew is that I wanted to please my parents. My goal was to move Washington D.C. and attend

Howard University and earn a Master's Degree in Psychology/Counseling. What I didn't know at the **TIME** is that the application for graduate school should have been submitted a semester earlier and I didn't meet the deadline. Pride is a powerful hindrance! I remained in DC and did not return to Pennsylvania. Instead, I went to work for a law firm as a receptionist and after hearing that Washington Hospital Center was hiring for an on-the-job training Respiratory Therapist, I applied. One of the needed requirements was to have a bachelor's degree, which I had. That job started my Respiratory Career. In two years, I returned to school and earned my Respiratory Therapy Degree. For 16 years I served as a Respiratory Therapist. The lesson to be learned here is, if God is trying to work something out in you and you continue to experience the same problems again and again regardless of who the persons are, at some point, you will find that it is not the people or the environment, but the problem is more likely YOU. Even though I kept missing the lesson and blaming other people, eventually, I got it. It was ME!

After I lost my Godmother to leukemia in 1992, my whole life took another turn, and I began grief counseling. Through continuous counseling, **TIME** allowed me to deal with my deep-rooted hurts experienced in my **TIME** of childhood. God then permitted me to join a local women's support group called MÁAT. I had a strong support of likeminded women who were willing to love me past my hurts, telling me the truth about me. My MÁAT sisters held me accountable for my decisions, actions, and choices.

Let me encourage you to look deep within yourself to be able to admit when **IT'S TIME** for true counseling. Make sure you have friends who will tell you the truth in love. Be sure your relationship with God is real, strong, and right. Be sure to balance your **TIME** both spiritually and naturally, be it work, church, family or fun time. After all, Ecclesiastes 3:1 says, "to everything there is a season, a **TIME** for every purpose under heaven."

Chapter 4
A Time to Process

Webster's dictionary defines process as a series of actions or steps taken in order to achieve a particular end. Here is what I know to be true, God is always working on our behalf behind the scenes, working all things out for our good according to Romans 8:28. Why? Because we love Him. I admit there were many times I did not know or understand what God was doing, nor did I understand why I had to go through certain things. Yet, I remember how the Apostle Paul asked the Lord three times to remove the thorn in his flesh" (2 Corinthians 12:8)…yes those times. For example, being rejected by members of the Church that disagreed with my Apostle ordaining me to be the Pastor of Givers of Life Ministries. Personally, I believe church hurt can feel like the worse hurt you could ever experience. I also believe that in the world you may expect the "heathen" to rage and turn against you, but you don't expect those that you labor with in the house of God to mistreat you, lie on you, and use you. There have even been times when mentors have turned on me for no apparent reason, joined my "haters" in talking about me. In my quiet time I cried out to the Lord and asked Him "why" He didn't removed the thorn of pain though but He could have. I found out that "His grace is sufficient for me" (2 Corinthians 12:9) even when church people and close family members hurt me.

Finally, there came a **TIME** when God spoke forgiveness and love from His Word according to Matthew 6:14-15. "If you forgive when they sin against you your heavenly father will also forgive you." His Word also says in John 13:34, as I have loved you, love one another. God also spoke to me and told me to always remember the cross. He told me I would never suffer the way he did on the cross. If he endured and forgave, certainly so can I. That is when he had me commit to memory Proverbs 16:7, “When a man’s ways please the Lord, he maketh even his enemies be at peace with him.” In my quiet **TIME,** God also had me meditate on Luke 6:32-36. That which was on my heart the most is, “If you love those who love you, what credit is that to you”…

During the healing process of **TIME** when God’s work was being done, it was very hard as well as uncomfortable. There were times I cried myself to sleep. This process was written in a journal along with the person's name whom I had to forgive by saying their name out loud. As I forgave each of them, I realized that they did not owe me anything! The more I surrendered to the process of forgiveness through **TIME,** it was then and only then did my healing begin. I didn’t know that the actual test would come when you could be in the same room with the person(s) who had hurt you and you don’t have a need to revisit the offense.

I once experienced someone who publicly asked me for my forgiveness, only to return three years later with the same offense and the threat of a physical altercation. What I didn't know at the time is that GOD allowed it all. In the **TIME** of this process God allowed me to realize he is the Alpha and Omega of all things. Often times God will allow the pain but bless God for allowing me to pass the test of forgiveness so that it no longer takes days, weeks, months, or years for me to do so. It's because I have been forgiven for much. "If you forgive those who sin against you, your heavenly Father will forgive you. But if you refuse to forgive others, your Father will not forgive your sins" (Matthew 6:14-15). In **TIME** I learned that hurting people hurt other people and I experienced both. Most brokenness begins in childhood and carries over into adulthood. If the brokenness or the dysfunction is never dealt with, it could cause the individual to grow up with low self-esteem, feelings of resentment, or rejection. Therefore, if you do or say certain things, it may trigger something that reminds them of that particular painful experience and causes them to relive that painful **TIME**. This healing process is shared freely that others may take **TIME** and allow God's process to begin in them, prayerfully through the writing of this book.

One of the examples of rejection as well as self-esteem issues came with my 5ft 10 inches in stature and my complexion. People called me "light skinned." Many times, there were those who did not remember my name. They referred to me as that tall light skinned woman. At times even my family members described me this way, so imagine how over **TIME** this created self-esteem issues for me. Yes, I have experienced this in the church, school, women conferences. and gatherings. Yet, our heavenly Father does not have respect of gender, color nationality or height. So I was grateful that my earthly father adored me enough to always call me beautiful, validating me as a princess in the making of a queen. Being created in His image and His likeness, God has truly persuaded me to operate in my queen like character. Giving much thanks to God who has blessed my level of confidence, being able to tap into my inheritance as an African American Queen, knowing that "all good and perfect gifts come from God..."(James 1:17). After all, it is God's good pleasure that we "prosper in all things and be in good health even as our soul prospers" (3 John 1:2). Everything I have comes from God! To God be the glory for the **TIME** and energy He allowed me to obtain education and degrees in Respiratory Therapy, Bachelor's in Psychology with a minor in Biology, and a Master's in Education Administration. God used my Father Blackwell to bless me financially.

The reason I mentioned this is because at times a spirit of jealousy will present itself along your journey. These spirits are designed to stop as well as block you...even inside of your inner circle there should be healthy boundaries. There are times when you may have to love people from a distance.

During this process of **TIME**, God delivered me. He delivered me from what they thought and their wrong perception of who I was. With my out -going personality I was never short of friends even after being hurt by some of them. God had put others in place to pray for me as He restored me.

In this process, God allowed **TIME** for self examination. Sometimes I would ask myself, am I reaping things I had sown, because there would be consequences for my inappropriate behavior. So grateful and thankful for God's mercy and grace because I realized my consequences could have been worse. I had to keep in mind that some people never forget the "old" Cynthia. However, the word of God says, "if anyone is in Christ, he is a new creation, old things have passed away, behold all things have become new" (2 Corinthians 5:17). In this process of **TIME**, you must be persistent and prayerful to what you hold dear and true. What I know is true is that God loves me, and I love God. I am reminded everyday of Jeremiah 29:11 which says, "for I know the thoughts I think towards you, says the Lord, thoughts of peace and not of evil, to give you a future and a hope." What I have learned, is that **IT'S TIME** to Trust the Lord completely and put our confidence in God, not in man. Know that in the process, you will be mistreated, misunderstood, lonely, lied on, and often rejected, but rest assured it will all work out for your good. All I have seen and experienced has allowed me to share my testimonies with you in hopes to encourage you to make it through your process. There is light at the end of the tunnel. People are in your life for a reason, a season, or a lifetime. Therefore, let us ask God to help us to discern people and seasons. **It's Time,** to go through the process and let patience have its perfect work.

Chapter 5
Time for Obedience

In 2000, God spoke to me and in obedience to what He had spoken, I learned it was **TIME** to change my career after 16 years as a Certified Respiratory Therapist. God opened the door to education. I became a teacher, later an Assistant Principal, as God would have it, I became a principal. Being obedient to God may have caused me to take a cut in salary, nevertheless, it was better to obey God knowing it would all work together for my good financially as well as spiritually. My point here is, there will be times when obedience causes you to be still for a **TIME** in order to be able to move forward in God's appointed **TIME**.

I am a living testimony and proof that God can do more with less when we obey. God blessed me to purchase my first home on a teacher's salary. This **TIME** of obedience revealed to me that it is not so much about what your salary is as it is about being a good steward with what God gives to you. Dealing with my needs and not my wants, I found myself saving a lot more and taking in roommates which was also a blessing. This caused me to re-examine myself by having others live with me. The advantage was that God taught me the purpose of saving money. It was in God's **TIME** that caused my goals to be met as well as my obedience.

When you have a real relationship with God and not just a form of Godliness there will be times He will speak to you about your place of fellowship, and where to sow your financial seed. The key is to listen and obey.

From my past experiences I have learned that God will only tell or give you in part what He wants from you. He wants you to be able to obey and master what He gives you in part before allowing you to see the bigger picture. When I asked God why he does that with me, He didn't answer for some time and then one day He showed me something and I was shocked and overwhelmed, even though it was something I had been praying and believing God would do for years. Truthfully, what God has for you is already done, but you must be ready and in position to receive it. I cried and said, "thank you" Jesus, I am so grateful and overwhelmed. In a still small voice I heard him say, "I know daughter, this is why I don't tell or show my children everything all at once. It will be overwhelming, and some may even become stagnated or fearful. God never gives His children more than they can handle."

Obedience to God is not always easy but is necessary. "Obedience is better than sacrifice" (1 Samuel 15:22). Obedience is connected to trust. We must trust God in every area of our lives, especially when you don't understand and cannot see our way. Faith is also necessary and is partnered with trust. "Without faith it is impossible to please God" (Hebrews 11:6) therefore, when the three dynamic trios (trust, faith, obedience) are operating in our lives it is impossible to be defeated. Know that obedience to God does not require approval from best friend, your spouse, prayer partner, coworker, boss or family member. Being obedient to God plays an important part in the process, your purpose and the blessing God has in store for you. God is not interested in emotionalism. He needs our hearts to be in relationship with Him because that relationship with Him will lead to our ability to trust Him, hear Him, have faith in Him, and be obedient to Him. Reading His word and applying biblical principles to our everyday lives is also important. Without biblical principles we would be lost. We must cherish our relationship with Him and the fact that he speaks to us, reveals things, and confirms spiritual and natural things to us. Seek God with your whole heart, pursue Him daily, and allow him to be Lord over your life. In **TIME** He will disconnect or connect you with the people you should have in your life. People will come into your life for a reason or season. Others may be for a lifetime but it's all up to God if you trust Him with faith to guide you. I caution you to monitor the people you surround yourself with...the ones in your network, your fellowship. Wrong company can hinder or stop your progress and block your blessings. Allow God to choose your friends and separate you from those who should not be in your season. Be obedient to his lead and don't spend time justifying the reason you are in friendships and relationships that are not good for you. Learn to let go and let God.

Sometimes, God wants to know that He can trust you with your money, trust you to tell people the truth in love and trust you to be transparent when you have fallen short of what He expects of you. Do you have a teachable and humble spirit? Many people want to be leaders without making the sacrifices God requires for the leading of His people. I'm speaking about humbleness, and patience, and process. If you struggle with apologizing and admitting when you are wrong, leadership is not for you. If you can't effectively communicate (requires listening too), leadership is not for you. If God is calling you in ministry, as a leader, can you be obedient, follow His lead, wait for His timing, be prepared to go through the process, and do not quit? Are you invested in keeping your eyes on God, fasting and praying on a regular basis?

Let me share a short testimony with you. I was serving as a leader in a small church as the Children's Church Coordinator. At one meeting the Pastor had us take a Spiritual Inventory test (I would highly recommend everyone to take this test). We were required to share the top 5 gifts with the entire class. I remember one of my five results came up as Pastor. I laughed hysterically! I wanted to take the test again. My Pastor said to me, "yes, I knew it, I saw it in you, but you are thinking it has to happen tomorrow." Please note it is a process and will happen over **TIME**. God is developing you in many areas of your life before this will actually come to pass. Now, let me be transparent, I left that meeting fired up mad! I told

God (yes, I said, I told God) that I just wanted to teach the children and be a part of Children's Church. I began to tell God all the reasons why I couldn't and didn't want to be a Pastor. I wrestled with the thought. I could never imagine a being Pastor. Well, as God would have it (not me), on July 1, 2012, I was ordained as a Pastor after spending years of wresting and reasoning with myself, comparing myself with others, including pastors. For years I had looked over my past sins, faults, and mistakes and disqualified myself. I had all the reasons why God should not have called me to Pastor. I could truly understand why Moses questioned God and informed him about his speech impediment (stuttering).

Here is where I want to encourage you. There will never be a **TIME** when God will make a mistake. What God has for you is for you! When God calls you, man can't disqualify you! They can talk about you and put obstacles in your way, but they cannot undo what God has already done, has already qualified and equipped you to do or be. "Before He formed you in the womb He knew you..."(Jeremiah 1:5).

Before, I end this chapter, let me caution you, don't allow circumstances and situations to cause you to surrender and be disobedient. Willingly accept Gods' call. Many of your blessings are contingent on your obedience. The situation that helped me surrender to the call of being a Pastor was when God spoke to me and told me He had called me to the five ministry gifts in Ephesians 4:11. I was hindering my Apostle from moving forward with assignments he had for her because I was operating in disobedience, because of fear and feelings of inadequacies. Trust me, we will never be fully equipped and adequate at anything. That would mean we would be perfect, so stop hiding behind fear and inadequacies. God will equip you in His timing for the work He has called you to do and when **IT'S TIME** to be obedient to His voice.

Chapter 6
No Time For Fear

In 2 Timothy 1:7 tells us “For God has not given us a spirit of fear, but of power and of love and of a sound mind.” Therefore, if fear is not of God then it must be from the devil. We can call those things that are not into existence (Romans 4:17). When fear tries to grab a hold of us, we can stop and say, “what did God say about this?" Then quote the word of God and bring it to life in our life. This is one of the many ways we can defeat fear.

I have heard two acronyms for fear (F=false, E=evidence, A=appearing, R=real, and F=face, E=everything, A=and, R=recovery). Many times, fear will cause us to avoid a circumstance or situation which is not always as bad as we think or make it, which is why it important to face and deal with uncomfortable situations, and why we have those unpleasant conversations. It's a matter of coming face to face with our fears so that we can defeat them and overcome them.

Fear will rob and destroy your future, your goals, peace, joy and relationships, (including marriages). Fear is a tormenting spirit. However, God does not want His sons and daughters living in fear. He created us to worship, praise Him and love Him. God wants us to prosper and be in good health. He does not want us living in fear of people, places, and things. 1 John 4:18 says, "There is no fear in love; but perfect love casts out fear, because fear involves torment. But he who fears has not been made perfect in love." God desires that we know perfect love. **IT'S TIME** to let go of your fears and walk in the freedom in which God has called and chosen for you. Be, careful, fear will attach itself to lies, worry and procrastination. This is not of God but of the devil who is "the father of lies" (John 8:44). When the devil begins speaking to your mind, recognize that whatever the devil is saying is the opposite of what God wants for you. He tried to convince me not to write this book because he said it would not sell. For years, I believed it and said, why bother when there are so many other good books out there that will encourage people. In my spirit God kept telling me to write this book. I began to look at my personal library, some were big books, some were small, some even had workbooks and guides for teaching. Within me, I too had a book that needed to be birthed, so here it is, birthed out in **IT'S TIME**!

Stop procrastinating. What do you really have to lose? "Just do it." I ask you, what is the devil lying to you about that has you living in fear? Somebody's life and deliverance are connected to your obedience; therefore, let go of your fear. What you are fearing could be somebody's answer. While they are praying to God, you have their answer, but you are allowing fear to stop and block you. Let go of the fear and obey God. It doesn't matter what it is. Don't let fear of the unknown cause you to miss out on something God has in store for you.

The next time the spirit of procrastination comes knocking at your door, don't answer. Respond by doing what you know you are supposed to do. Don't let fear, procrastination, or lies, hinder your blessings. You were created to do what God has placed in your heart to do. Nobody else can do your God given assignment. If God gave you the vision, the provision will be made available to you in God's **TIME**. Don't allow the fear of your past (choices, decisions, and mistakes) cause you not to move forward. God is a God of a second, third, fourth, and many chances. Grace and Mercy are on your side and new every day. REPENT and move forward. Overcoming fear of the unknown is having Faith in Jesus Christ. Fear is the opposite of faith. You can't have both. So, choose to have Faith, the results are endless. **IT's TIME, let go of the FEAR.**

Chapter 7
No Time For Failure

What is failure? Failure has been defined as a lack of success or **failing** to perform a duty or expected action. We have all had our failures at some **TIME** in life. However, having failed at one thing could cause us to be successful at another. It may have been a relationship, job you didn't get or couldn't do, a school exam, sporting event, a driving test, a business venture, or even communication with others that didn't turn out well. Perhaps, you attempted to lose weight or save a certain amount of money within a certain period of **TIME**. Maybe, you desired to purchase your first house or car, but the expected end fell through.

Failure is never a good feeling for any of us. It can cause us to feel shame and embarrassment. Sometimes those feelings may be hard to shake over time or perhaps you were the one that failure ignited a light within. As a result you attempted to try and try again finding the strength not to give up all together and in **TIME** rise above that failure.

I have learned the acronym for fail is (F=first, A=attempt, I=in, L=learning). Therefore, what can we learn from this acronym? The first attempt doesn't have to be the only attempt. Growth in our desire to do better the next time, with better preparation or learning to accept assistance, without being prideful, knowing that there is nothing wrong with seeking help. Did failure show you something about yourself that you need to change rather than to mask it through the years? Don't worry, there is a silver lining in all of this. After all, as human beings we will make mistakes and miss the mark because we are not perfect and failure is a part of life. Many will fail at something, probably more than once. Perhaps you may have to ask yourself why, what could you have done differently? Did you pray for God's guidance and instructions? Be honest with yourself about your failure. Learn from it, grow from it, try again if you have the opportunity. Be open in your honesty to the fact that whatever it was may have not been meant for you or at least at that **TIME**. Don't be so quick to blame others even though you may have allowed others to have a part in your failure...own your part and forgive. Communication and trust are crucial but, when it's all said and done it's really just between you and God.

In order to change and move forward, you must be willing to examine your life, choices, and decisions. Be teachable, have the right attitude, and learn to take one day at a **TIME**. I heard someone say, "pray about everything and worry about nothing." Trust God's timing, answers, and direction for your life. He promised he would never leave you or forsake you (Hebrews 13:5). He knows what is always best for you.

As I look back over my life, I see the times when I failed. I see how discouraged I became, the times I quit and the times I got back up. Those failures have allowed me to persevere and even write this book. I failed in relationships with men, family members, students and co-workers. I failed budgeting money, losing weight, and the loss of my basketball career due to an injury. Sometimes we fail because of people and circumstances. I failed in that capacity too. The key is through those failures God has made me wiser and stronger. In **TIME** because I didn't quit, I got back up, learned from my failure, matured and allowed God to help me overcome the shame, defeat, and embarrassment of it all.

I am at the point in my life, if I can help somebody by sharing my flaws or mistakes to help them avoid or overcome going down the same path I journeyed, then my living is not in vain. God will allow us to connect with people either to be a blessing or receive a blessing. Who knows, the blessing that may come from a failure that we may have experienced will help someone else. **IT'S TIME** that we change our perspective concerning our failures. Don't be the person that holds you back. **IT'S TIME** to rise to the occasion and let your past failures drive you towards your future success, a future waiting for you to receive the blessings God has for you.

Let it all go! Your goals and dreams may be delayed but not denied. God is waiting for YOU. Quit holding yourself up. **IT'S TIME** to exhale. **IT'S TIME** to try and begin again. That goes for the person who wants to lose weight, get re-married, find another job, change their careers, go back to school, to earn a degree, save money, perhaps buy a house, start a business, work in ministry or travel. **IT'S TIME, IT'S TIME, IT'S TIME**!

Chapter 8
A Time of Forgiveness

Forgiveness is not the easiest topic for many people to discuss or act upon. When someone has hurt you and or abused you, physically and or sexually, lied on you, mistreated and or neglected you, it wounds your soul. It is hard to forgive, let alone forget. However, the word of God says "If your brother or sister sins against you, rebuke them; and if they repent, forgive them. Even if they sin against you seven times in a day and seven times come back to you saying "repent" forgive them (Luke 17:3-4). Ephesians 4:32 say's be kind, and be compassionate to one another, and forgiving each other, just as Christ forgave you.

What is important for all of us to remember is that God has forgiven us for so many things and if you do not forgive others of their sins, your heavenly Father will not forgive you for your sins (Matthew 6:14-15).

The opposite of forgiveness is unforgiveness. When left to fester, unforgiveness can turn into bitterness and hatred. At that point it becomes poisonous to your soul, body and mind, and can or will affect your health. Unforgiveness is like a toxic chemical that destroys you and leaves you emotionally wounded and scarred. Have you ever heard of the statement, "hurting people hurt other people?"

Forgiveness has nothing to do with the person (people) who hurt you, however, it is all about you. Think about this, Jesus Christ being our greatest example. He was crucified on the cross, bled, died and hung there so that you and I could have eternal life. He was without sin...sinless, and yet he died for our sins and forgave those who persecuted, mocked him and hung him on the cross.

Let me be clear, I am not saying overlook the people who hurt you, nor am I saying what they did was not wrong. However, the bible says "...vengeance is mine, I will repay says the Lord" (Romans 12:19) and he will. He takes care of us all. "God is no respecter of person" (Romans 2:11). I often hear people say what goes around comes around. I am a true believer. Everybody reaps what they sow (Galatians 6:7) we will all have to give an account for what we have said and done which includes both good and bad deeds.

Forgiving the person(s) who hurt you, is not always easy. There are so many things that could remind you of the offense that cause you to relive the hurt all over again. Every **TIME** you see the offender, revisit a certain place, event or share time and space with them, it brings back memories, emotions, feelings and regrets. The key to forgiveness is to let go of past hurt and offenses and not allow them to continue to torment your mind by allowing the enemy to make them a constant reminder.

There are several ways we can choose to forgive. One way is to engage in a face-to-face conversation with the person. Another way is to write a letter to the person or when the person has passed you can speak forgiveness with a sincere heart. This all may be painful, but God will not put more on you than you can bear (1 Corinthians 10:13). You get free through that act of forgiveness...free of hurt, anger, or bitterness. "But if you do not **forgive**, neither will your Father in heaven **forgive** your trespasses" (Mark 11:26).

It is very difficult for some more than others to forgive. As victims we may feel the person should pay for the hurt they caused. Sometimes we may think, if I forgive them, they walk away free and are not accountable for the pain they caused. Although this kind of thinking can hurt us for years...it's better to forgive.

On two separate occasions, two different family members got a hold of my social security number, used it to open and apply for credit cards and left me with the bill. I had to make the decision to press charges. Needless to say, I was shocked, angry and hurt to have been a victim of identity theft, to add insult to injury, not only was it family, but I, the victim was being treated as if I had done something wrong.

Greed, jealousy, envy and hurt will cause people (including family members) to engage in inappropriate behavior. The right thing to do was to forgive them. It was a process. During that **TIME**, I cried, went to counseling, spoke to my pastor, told my best friend and members of my support group and all of them said the same thing, "Forgive and Forgive." They were all willing to listen to my hurt and pain, but if I am to be honest, some of them I avoided and didn't talk to for a long period of **TIME**. That was because I wanted another response. I wanted an AMEN partner, someone to agree with my bitter, hurting self. I wanted to be justified to take my own vengeance or if I really had to let God do it, I wanted to know it and see it. That's my truth...I was hurting and my heart was not right, God gave me grace to heal my pain. He knew he had great plans for me. He knew He was going to call me to be a Pastor. He knew my hurts would help to heal others that would go through the same hurts as I suffered.

During one of my counseling sessions my counselor reminded me that although I had been hurt by my family member (at the time, it was only one incident). I had also hurt other people. The challenge for me was to think about the people I had hurt and make amends by reaching out to apologize and ask for their forgiveness. This included church members, family members, co-workers and ex-boyfriends. I can tell you, I left that counseling session ANGRY and thinking, how dare that counselor give me such a homework assignment. I canceled my next two sessions and refused to go back. My anger was getting out of control, and it turned into bitterness. I was bothered by everyone and everything. I needed a deliverance and fast! I cried out to the Lord (Jesus) and began to revisit the suggestion of my counselor. I started calling and writing people... asking them to forgive me. In the beginning it was hard, but I wanted PEACE. I wanted to be FREE and DELIVERED. It didn't matter anymore what people might say about me. I was determined to get free so if that took forgiveness, then that's the path I was willing to take.

When I went to work, I started apologizing to doctors, nurses and coworkers. People actually began to think I was mental. My supervisor called me and asked was everything ok, did I need to take some **TIME**. I said, "no" I'm okay, in fact I am better than okay, I have been walking in unforgiveness for years concerning the people who have hurt me but now it was **TIME** for me to forgive the people I had hurt. It felt good taking my life back from those who had hurt me! I was bitter and angry for far too long and now I was gaining back my freedom and independence in only a few weeks after I had done the work of forgiveness. God opened doors for me.

From that point, I made it a point to practice being quick to forgive. I returned to counseling. When my counselor saw me, she smiled and said, "you have learned how to forgive and have fulfilled your homework assignment, now you are ready to deal with the anger." This too was a process. Keep in mind all the while I am professing to be a born-again Christian who truly loves the lord, goes to church Sunday after Sunday and bible studies every week. I was a walking talking time bomb ready to explode at any time if someone said or did something that I did not like. It didn't matter if they were my supervisors, co-workers, at the bank, the grocery store, driving, yet God loved me so much during this **TIME** that He allowed a Pastor to teach a series on "Anger is a Choice." I was now working through the process to conquer the anger and right at the end of this journey I found out that a second family member had stolen my identity. When I confronted them, they were not truthful and anger wanted to rise up in me all over again, but this **TIME** I responded differently by using the strategies given to me by my counselor as well as the notes I had taken while my Pastor taught on this topic. I quickly forgave this person and moved on. I wasn't stuck like I was before. Love really does and will cover a multitude of sin. God is so funny how he uses our life stories to help others! He sends people to my Church who struggle with anger, unforgiveness, now I am able to immediately recognize it or they confess it and God allows me to minister to them. I now think it is awesome how he allowed me to experience those family members sabotaging my credit, character, and identity. Through it all, I learned how to love and forgive. As a result, God can trust and use me to minister to others. Our God is awesome! That's why I have learned to trust God and trust the process. He knows how much we can bear.

Whatever trial or test you have gone through; God wants to use you in that particular area. He wants to get all the glory from your life. He wants you to walk in forgiveness. Let people off the hook including yourself. You will in turn be free and liberated to be used as a vessel for God to free and liberate others.

Before I end this chapter on forgiveness, I want to mention one more thing. Through this process of forgiving, it is very important that you forgive yourself. Accept the areas in which you have made mistakes due to poor choices or immaturity. You can't go back to fix or change it. However, you can forgive yourself without the escape of overeating, over shopping, gambling, sexing, or other inappropriate behaviors or things you indulge in to suppress your feelings. Forgive and love yourself. **IT'S TIME TOFORGIVE.**

Chapter 9
Time For Positive Thinking

"For as a man thinketh in his heart so is he" (Proverbs 23:7). This is a powerful statement. Whatever you think ends up manifesting. You know why? When you think on a thought long enough, you will begin to speak it and when you put it in the atmosphere that is when it will happen. Therefore, are you putting negativity into the atmosphere or positivity? For you to turn negative into a positive, you must condition your thoughts to be positive. In Philippians 4:8 says "Finally, brethren, whatever things are true, whatever things are noble, whatever things are just, whatever things are pure, whatever things are lovely, whatever things are a good report, if there is any virtue and if there is anything praiseworthy-meditate on these things." Where do negative thoughts come from?

From a toxic environment, dysfunctional family issues, a negative or inappropriate experience can become embedded in our spirit. **IT'S TIME** for healing and hope! **IT'S TIME** for honesty **IT'S TIME** to change our way of thinking, changing from negative to positive that these two will manifest in and through us. **IT'S TIME** for the posture of positive to happen.

For 21 days think and write about things for which you are grateful. This assignment will help assist you to be grateful. The more grateful you are, the less likely you are to think negative. Two opposing forces cannot occupy the same space. You are either going to think negative or positive, be grateful or ungrateful. Gratitude will produce a positive fruit of thanksgiving. You can't complain and praise at the same **TIME**. Let us be careful not to complain, considering that perhaps this **TIME** someone is now experiencing some sort of trauma or tragedy far worse. Let us count the small blessings as well as those bigger than life that God has given. Change what you are saying and putting into the atmosphere, choose your words very carefully. Be transformed in your mind. Whatever is in the mind transforms to the heart and eventually will come out of the mouth. This is why God said, "death and life are in the power of the tongue" (Proverbs 18:21). Beloved I pray that after reading this book, especially this chapter, you will have a great desire to change. Change is a process that takes patience, prayer, and the forgiveness of oneself.

The next time you find yourself thinking negative, immediately dismiss the thought and command your mind to line up and focus on positive things. Don't be ashamed or afraid to get an accountability partner with whom you can confess your struggles and weakness, asking them to show and tell you when you are speaking negative. No matter what areas of your life you are working on, it all requires work that will not happen overnight. Therefore, think about it. What strategies can or will you use to change those negative thinking patterns? Don't be ashamed or afraid to go to God and tell him what you need. "If we confess our sins, he is faithful and just to forgive us our sins, and to cleanse us from all unrighteousness" (I John 1:9).

In order to think positive, we must have positive insight to what we see or hear...people, places and things. We must protect our eye gate (what we are watching), protect our ear gate (what or who are we listening to) and who is influencing you or what kind of company you are keeping. Are you being influenced by like minded people who are getting the same spiritual nourishment as you?

I have numerous friends that come from different backgrounds and religions. In my friendships, we encourage and support each other. We don't always agree on everything, but our relationships are based on love, truth and respect. When I was younger and immature, I chose friends that I thought would always agree with me and be my AMEN partner. As I began to change and work on Cynthia, I realized I needed women in my life that would tell me truth and love me in spite of my past and mistakes.

Encouraging people to think positive helped me get a perspective on my, life giving me the courage to write this book. It was essential for me to take that leap of faith. I want people to be free and spiritually liberated and walking in their God given purpose knowing that God loves them. **IT'S TIME** for us as people of God to stop allowing the enemy of our souls to steal our peace and love and no longer to be hindered from healthy relationships. **IT'S TIME** for positive thinking. Let God's Word speak to your mind through His holy instructions. He is a mind regulator.

IT'S TIME TO THINK POSITIVE

Roman 12:2

"And do not be conformed to this world, but be transformed by the renewing of your mind, that you may prove what *is* that good and acceptable and perfect will of God."

Isaiah 26:3

You will keep him in perfect peace,
whose mind is stayed on You,
Because he trusts in You."

Philippians 2:5

"Let this mind be in you which was also in Christ Jesus"...

Chapter 10
Time For Motivation

Motivation is the process that initiates, guides and maintains goal-oriented behavior. Motivation involves the biological, emotional, social and cognitive forces that activate behavior. What motivates you? Is it a person/people, place or object? Maybe you don't have anyone or anything to motivate you. Let me encourage you to dream and pursue your destiny. What is your greatest passion? Let us consider that life is too short, and tomorrow is not promised to any of us, the truth of the matter is, you have more days behind you than you have ahead of you. Trust God with the rest of your **TIME.** He will be your greatest motivator for moving towards your purpose and passion.

As I mentioned earlier, I have some awesome amazing girlfriends (some single, some married) and we encourage and motivate each other. You must understand there is a **TIME** and a season for everything. I pray this book will motivate and encourage many. I was inspired to write this book as a motivation for those who would read this book. There are so many books out there that can motivate you including the Holy Bible which is God's Word. **IT'S TIME** to know that "you can do all things through Christ who strengthens you" (Philippians 4:13). What I learned through my experiences of being a Pastor and Principal is, I can be someone's motivation. God has equipped me with compassion, wisdom, love, faith and education to help others. My belief in God and consistent prayer life encourages me to trust Him that He will lead and guide my conversations, footsteps, and relationships. It has been my experience that people are in our lives for a reason or a season. Either we are to deposit something into them or receive something from them. Humility and having a teachable spirit are crucial to our success as individuals and leaders.

Whatever you are passionate about pray about it, let God lead and guide you. **IT'S TIME**.

Chapter 11
Distractions of Time

Distractions, distractions, many distractions! Distraction is a thing that prevents someone from giving full attention to something else. It can be more than one thing distracting you. Distractions can be people, objects, places and things. Social Media can be a great distraction. Your job can be a distraction. Gossiping can be a distraction. Dealing with sickness and disease of oneself or a love one can be a distraction.

I am a firm believer that acquiring self control, along with wisdom and knowledge will assist in recognizing when distractions is trying to take you off course in any endeavor. One thing for sure there are 24 hours in a day, 7 days in a week and 365 days in a year unless it is a leap year. During the duration of **TIME**, it is crucial that we live a balanced life. Balanced meaning, we keep God at the center of our lives and seek him first before all else. We love our family and spend quality **TIME** with them. We attend church and church functions, go to work, school, have fun, rest and relax. Every day is not going to be peaches and cream. There will be some good days, bad days, ups and downs, joy and pain. Regardless of what is going on, let us keep moving forward, not allowing test and trials to cause us to stop trusting and believing in God. We must keep our faith and priorities.

There is nothing wrong with being a good listener however, you are neither responsible to take on another person's problem or pain. I have observed too many people going through unnecessary drama that have caused them to be burdened, simply because they took on another person's issues. Whenever something goes on such as confusion, arguments, disagreements, I say to myself let me mind my own Blackwell business. As much as possible I stay in my own lane and deal with my stuff. As a leader, I am often pulled into situations. I refuse to be a controlling leader but one of example. My point is, don't allow other people's problems to become yours problem and walk around thinking you need to have an answer for everyone's problem. That can be stressful, burdensome, and definitely a distraction. Distractions can hinder your progress. If left unchecked, distractions can be your enemy. Anything working against you is your enemy. However, you have control over who you associate with as well as what you say out of your mouth. Be mindful of where you spend your time, space, and money.

Some examples of distractions are spending money you don't have especially when you are trying to save. Another example can be going out to eat with friends after you worked hard to cut back on certain kinds of food and drinks. In this instance not only the food but the comments of friends can be a distraction.

In order for a person to understand their distractions they must be willing to identify what distracts them and take the necessary action. This could mean not going to the restaurant where I might be tempted of hanging out with people who comment instead of applauding my self-control.

My experience has been sharing your plans and where you are in your life with others is not always the wisest choice.

It's up to you to identify the things, places and people that are distracting you. Make choices to set up healthy boundaries that cause you not to be distracted.

I want to end this chapter by encouraging people to be alert and watch for those things that cause distractions and hinder your progress with God, especially during a **TIME** of prayer and fasting. When we pray and or read the bible, distractions come in many forms. However, the word of God says, if you resist the devil he must flee (James 4:7).

Anything or anybody that comes to steal your joy and peace is a distraction. You may need a season of separation. This is your **TIME** be an overcomer.

Chapter 12
Time to Heal

Psalms 107:20 declares "He sent His word and healed them." I truly believe the healing we receive from God has no limitations whether it is physical, mental, spiritual, or emotional. Mental healing is just as important as physical healing when we experience sicknesses such as cancer, COVID 19, diabetes or high blood pressure. God says in Jeremiah 30:17 "For I will restore health to you and heal you and your wounds..."

God wants us to be healthy and whole. Therefore, we must be healed in our soul, spirit, and body. The soul is made up of our emotions, will, and mind. The Spirit of God in you is that part of the natural man that connects you to God. Take your inventory and if you are lacking in the soul, spirit, and body, I recommend that you seek Doctor Jesus. He can heal and deliver the spirit, mental and physical, and the good thing about Doctor Jesus is that it's free. The price has already been paid when He went to the cross. There is no co-pay, and He doesn't misdiagnosis. The initial consult with Doctor Jesus consists of you confessing and admitting you have an issue. There is nothing to hard for Doctor Jesus.

I don't know if some people realize just how important your mind and conversations will affect your life, actions and health.

Over the years I have learned that stress is your enemy. Stress can cause organs in your body to weaken, affect your immune system, cause you to lose hair and sleep. God did not design our bodies to be stressed. Therefore, it is so important to cast every care and burden on God because he cares for us (I Peter 5:7). Jesus didn't die on the cross for us to be stressed, have anxiety, panic attacks, suffering with depression, with all manner of diseases or pains. All those are tricks of the enemy designed to keep you defeated, distracted and away from a relationship with God and His love. However, as you read this book, I decree and declare that everyone who is struggling or have struggled with a mental illness, spiritual, physical issues will be delivered and set free right now, in the name of Jesus, never again be entangled with those spirits that have come to attack your mind, body, spirit, and soul. It is my prayer that you will walk in your deliverance and healing because God has set you free and who the Son sets free is free INDEED (John 8:36).

Jehovah Rapha is the Lord God that heals us and according to Psalms 107:20 God sent His word and it healed us. Let me pause right here... it doesn't matter why you may need healing or deliverance. For some it may be physical, others it may be mental, emotional or the healing of a broken heart...one of separation or divorce. Regardless of the healing I want you to be encouraged because Psalms 147:3 says, "Many are the afflictions of the righteous, but the Lord delivers them out of them all."

If you are reading this book and know without a shadow of a doubt you need healing, then as I pray this healing confession may it manifest in your life. You can also pray this pray with me.

My Daily Healing Confession

Father in the Name of Jesus, your word decrees and declares according to Jeremiah 30:17 you will restore health and healing to me and heal me of my wounds (announce the healing). I take authority over every symptom and hindering spirits that has been sent on assignment to cause me to be in pain and doubt that you can or will heal me. Jesus you are my great High Priest, and you are hearing my confession and I am and will hold fast to this confession of Faith.

(Insert your name here) is healed by the stripes of Jesus. Jesus carried (Insert your name here) sickness and infirmities. In the name of Jesus (Insert your name here) cast out all spirits of infirmity that would attack (Insert your name here) body. (Insert your name here) speaks healing and strength to my bones, muscles, skin, joint, organs, mind, eyes, throat, glands, blood marrow, immunity & nervous systems, lungs, kidneys, liver, spleen, spine, pancreas, bladder, ears, nose, sinuses, mouth, tongue, feet, high blood pressure, diabetes, ulcers, tumors, dementia, head, Alzheimer's, cancer, depression, mental illnesses, seizures, Crohn's disease, Lupus, Sarcoidosis, Auto Immunity Disorder, in the name of Jesus. (Insert your name here) prospers and walks in health even as (Insert your name here) prospers.

(Insert your name here) is fearfully and wonderfully made. Let my body function in the wonderful way you designed it to function. I am being healed as I make my confession known this day. I believe and receive my supernatural healing; it is so In Jesus Name. AMEN.

IT'S TIME for you to be healed and walk in your healing in your spirit, soul, and body.

Chapter 13
Time for Transparency

Transparency often involves, "communication, openness, and accountability." It is my thought that the reason why many people are not as transparent as they could or would like to be is because they are afraid of what people will think or say. The bible encourages us that no man without sin should cast a stone at another (John 8:7). In addition, Romans 3:23 says, "for all have sinned and fall short of the glory of God." We all have sinned. In addition, we were all shaped in iniquity and born into sin (Psalm 51:5). This is the reason why nobody has a right to judge or talk about anyone. Let me be transparent about this. I myself have been guilty of gossiping and talking about someone or something.

In my transparency, everyday, I first strive to daily please my heavenly father and then also my natural father, as long as they are pleased, I am good. Prayerfully, soon I will be married so I will add pleasing my future husband to the list. It is my prayer that you will love yourself and make peace with your past and others. **IT'S TIME** to be transparent enough to just love yourself and God. There is nothing wrong with being confident.

Let me take this time to encourage you. Don't allow others to limit your expectations or what you want to accomplish.

I have not always made the right choices, but I am so grateful and thankful for the grace of God. Being in transparency posture means we are able to admit that we have failed and done things shameful while we are on this Christian journey. I understand what it takes to be transparent because of some the things I have had to endure and overcome. Through my counseling I have been able to gain coping skills to overcome my dysfunctional behaviors and my dysfunctional relationships. In **TIME**, God's grace, mercy, love and forgiveness has been extended to me as well as to you. There are no secrets with God. We are all transparent before Him.

God desires true honesty and holiness. He is not a God of secrets. The key to transparencies success is to repent daily. As God's leader, transparency with God's people should be a priority. May I take this time to encourage those who may be living with secrets and embarrassed about your past choices and decisions, **IT'S TIME** to surrender it all to God, be transparent. Don't be ashamed to tell your testimony, it will help others overcome.

I have love in my heart for everyone. I am a giving person. Speaking transparently when I find myself in error, God chastises me, and I repent. Repentance is turning away from the error. Jesus died on the cross and we are redeemed from the curse of the enemy. Do not let people define you by your past choices as you make the decision to be transparent. This is being confident in your salvation and spiritual walk with God. You see, I believe God and choose to serve God with all my heart. **IT'S TIME** for us to please God! Will we fail, will we miss the mark, of course we will because we are but flesh. God wants us to strive to be Christ like, to have the mind of Christ. Therefore, daily repentance is necessary and a daily prayer life and relationship with Jesus is crucial.

In my closing I give you this testimony. I had desired to write a book since 2009. It is now August 2021 and I finally stopped procrastinating and started writing this book, although many issues, hindrances, and deliverances needed to take place before the writing could begin. Twelve years later here is the finished product. After all, **IT'S TIME.**

Conclusion

Well, I did it. I wrote and published my first book. I said a lot and dropped some nuggets here and there. It is now **TIME** for you to apply what you read to your life.

I pray you have been encouraged, inspired, motivated, and have surrendered to God, to do and be what he has called you to do according to the plan He has for you (Jeremiah 29:11).

IT'S TIME for us to possess what God has destined for each of us. God said, in 3 John 2, "Beloved, I pray that you may prosper in all things and be in health, just as your soul prospers" (NKJV). Take one day at a time. Stay focused on what you need to do and when necessary, say "NO" as God leads you. Keep healthy boundaries with friends and family. Be persistent to the end. Trust God and you will accomplish your goals and dreams. **IT'S TIME.**

Closing Prayer

I can't assume that everyone that reads this book is saved and believes in or knows how to accept our Lord and Savior Jesus Christ into their lives. I offer you the chance to do that now by praying this prayer: Father God in the name of Jesus, I believe that according to John 3:16 that you loved me so much that you provided forgiveness for my sins through the death of your Son Christ Jesus. Come into my life and heart as my personal Lord and Savior. I believe that according to Luke 19:10 you came to seek and save those that are lost and I confess I am lost without you. I know that I do not have to be ashamed because Romans 3:23 tells me that "all have sinned and fallen short of your glory." Thank you for dying on the cross for my past, present and future sins. I believe you are the way the truth and the light according to John 14:6.

Thank you for eternal life. Thank you that I am a new creature and old things have passed away according to 2 Corinthians 5:17 "and all things have become new."

If you repeated that prayer, you are a new creation in the family of God. I encourage you to pray to God (just talking to him from your heart) and ask him to direct you to a church where you can fellowship and assemble with other believers (Hebrews 10:25). Be teachable, learn of His truth by participating in bible studies so you can grow in the knowledge of God.

Notes

Notes (continued)

Endnotes

Introduction

1. Definition of Time. *Google Apps*.

Chapter 1:

1. See Ecclesiastes 3: 1-8
2. See Romans 8:28
3. Refer to John 3:16
4. Refer to John 10:28-30
5. See Luke 19:19
6. See Proverbs 18:21
7. Anger is a Choice by Tim LaHaye
8. 30 Days To Taming Your tongue by Deborah Pegues

Chapter 2:

1. Refer to Genesis 1:1
2. Refer to John 1: 1-4
3. Journey to the Kingdom of God by Shelby Walker

Chapter 4:

1. Process defined, Webster's Dictionary –*Google apps*
2. Refer to Proverbs 16:7

3. Refer to Luke 6:32
4. See Matthew 6: 14-15
5. Refer to III John 2
6. Refer to James 1:17

Chapter 5

1. Refer to Isaiah 55:8
2. See Hebrews 11:6
3. Refer to Jeremiah 1:5
4. Refer to Ephesians 4:11

Chapter 6

1. See II Timothy 1:7
2. See Romans 4:17
3. See John 8:44

Chapter 7

1. Definition of Fear , *Google apps*

Chapter 8

1. Refer to Luke 17:3-4
2. Refer to Ephesians 4:32
3. Refer to Matthew 6:14-15
4. See Romans 12:19
5. See Galatians 6:7-8

Chapter 9

1. Refer to Proverbs 23:7

2. Refer to Philippians 4:6
3. Refer to I John 1:19

Chapter 10

1. Define Motivation, *Google Apps*

Chapter 11

1. See James 4:7

Chapter 12

1. Refer to Psalms 107:20
2. Refer to Jeremiah 30:17
3. Refer to Peter 5:7
4. Refer to Psalms 33:19

Chapter 13

1. Transparency Definition, *Google Apps*
2. Refer to John 8:7
3. Refer to Romans 3:23
4. See Psalms 51:5
5. See Proverbs 15:1
6. See Psalms 103:1

Conclusion

1. See Jeremiah 29:11
2. See II John 2

Closing Prayer

1. See John 3:16
2. See Luke 19:10
3. See Romans 8:32
4. See John 14:6
5. See II Corinthians 5:17

IT'S TIME

By Pastor Cynthia Blackwell

Published by 1 accord Christian
Publishing Ministry

1accordcpm@gmail.com
202 - 774-9944

Made in the USA
Middletown, DE
02 June 2022